WHO LIVED HERE?

My Victorian Home

KAREN BRYANT-MOLE

WATTS BOOKS
LONDON · NEW YORK · SYDNEY

© 1995 BryantMole Books

Published by
Watts Books
96 Leonard Street
London EC2A 4RH

Franklin Watts Australia
14 Mars Road
Lane Cove
NSW 2066

UK ISBN: 0 7496 1961 9
Dewey Decimal Classification Number: 941.081

10 9 8 7 6 5 4 3 2 1

A CIP catalogue record for this book is available from the British Library.

Design and illustration: Chrissie Sloan
Photographer: Zul Mukhida

Consultant: Rosemary Allan,
Senior Keeper and Keeper of Social History, Beamish,
The North of England Open Air Museum

Acknowledgements
The author and publisher would like to thank the Page family for allowing us to base this book
on their Victorian home.
Photographs: Beamish, The North of England Open Air Museum 4 (both), 5 (both), 8, 11
(bottom), 13 (top), 15 (top), 17 (bottom), 19 (both), 21, 23 (top), 25 (both), 27 (both), 29
(both), Chapel Studios 11 (top), 13 (bottom), 17 (top), 23 (bottom).

Printed in Malaysia

Contents

Some of the more difficult words are explained on page 31.

The Victorians

The word 'Victorian' is used to describe people and objects that were around at the time that Queen Victoria was queen of Great Britain and Ireland.

Victoria became queen when she was only eighteen years old, in 1837. That's about 160 years ago. She was on the throne for nearly 65 years, until she died in 1901. So, anything that was made or anyone who lived between 1837 and 1901 could be called Victorian. It is also called the Victorian Age or the Victorian Era.

Inventions

There were lots of changes to everyday life during the Victorian Era. Many of these changes were a result of new inventions. Telephones, sewing machines, motor cars and typewriters are just a few of the many Victorian inventions.

Railway engines

One of the most important inventions was the railway engine. Before the railways, horses and canals were the only way of taking goods and people from one part of the country to another. This was slow and expensive. The railways made travel quicker and cheaper.

Factories

Many factories were built during the Victorian Age. The factories needed workers, like the men in this photograph. More and more people moved into the towns to work in the factories and do all sorts of other jobs. These people needed houses. Huge numbers of houses were built during the Victorian era.

This book will tell you about one Victorian house.

My Home

This house was built in 1895. It could be called Late Victorian because it was built near the end of Queen Victoria's reign.

There are lots of things about the house that show you it is Victorian.

Instead of seeing brickwork on the outside of the house, the bricks have been covered with smooth plaster. This is called stucco.

Many Mid to Late Victorian homes were stuccoed.

The main windows are bay windows. This means they come forwards in a sort of box shape, with extra windows down the side. Some Victorian houses had bay windows, others did not.

All the windows are a type called sash windows. They come in two sections. The top part can be pulled down and the bottom part pushed up. Their name comes from the rope or sash cord that runs inside the window frame.

Not everything about this house is the same as when it was built. The modern tiles on the roof are made from concrete. The original tiles would have been slate or clay tiles.

Here are the Page family. They are the people who now live in the house. Laurie is the youngest.

Behind him you can see his elder brother, Sam, and his mum, Jan.

You will discover more about Laurie, his family and their Victorian home, as you read through this book.

Before you turn the page, look for a small brown knob on the edge of the door surround. You will find out what this is on page 11.

The First Owners

The people who first lived in this house were called the Brown family. Mr Brown was a builder. In fact Mr Brown built this house and most of the other houses in the street!

Mr and Mrs Brown had three children. There were two girls, called Vera and Lily, and a baby boy called Thomas. Two other people lived in the house with the Browns. They were Thomas's nanny and their maid, whose name was Mary.

Terraces

Towards the end of the Victorian Age, more and more homes were needed in the towns. Builders bought plots of land. On the plots of land they built groups of houses that were joined together.
A group of houses that is joined together is called a terrace. Some Victorian terraces stretched from one end of the street to the other. Others were built in blocks of four or five houses. The Browns' house was the last to be built in a terrace of five houses.

Instead of using an architect to design each house, builders usually worked from a sort of pattern book. These pattern books mean that lots of Victorian houses look very similar.

These drawings show you the plan of the downstairs and the upstairs of the Browns' house. You can look at the plans as you read the book. It will help you to work out where you are in the house.

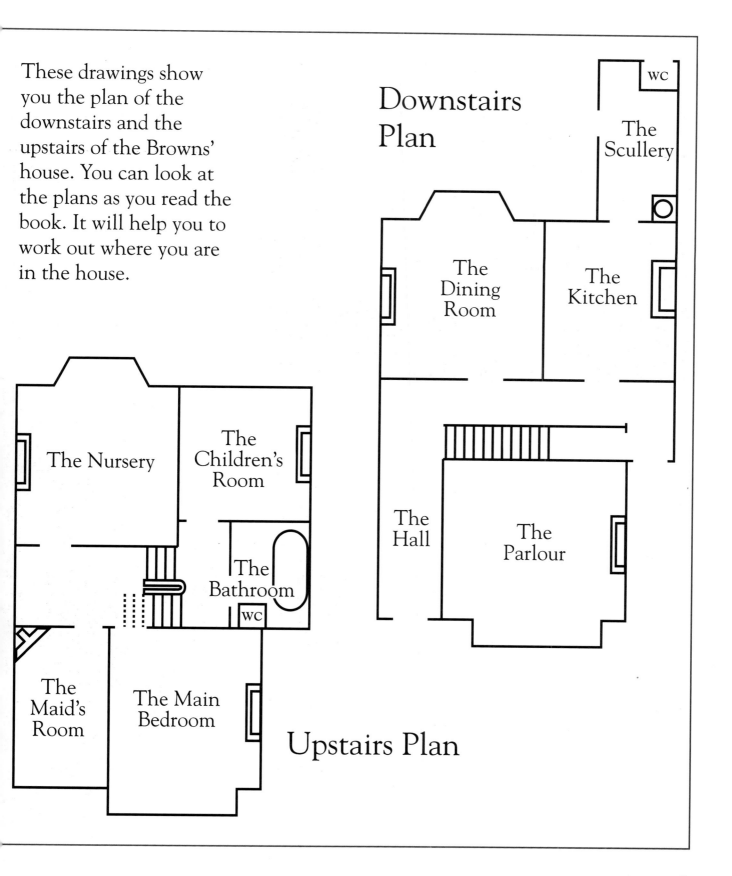

Downstairs Plan

WC

The Scullery

The Dining Room

The Kitchen

The Hall

The Parlour

The Nursery

The Children's Room

The Bathroom

WC

The Maid's Room

The Main Bedroom

Upstairs Plan

The Hall

This picture shows you what the hall looks like now. Can you see that Laurie has left his mountain bike by the front door?

Most of the woodwork in Laurie's hall is painted white. But the Browns would probably have painted the woodwork dark brown. The Victorians liked dark, rich colours. Their wallpapers were often deep shades of red or green.

The hall was a very important part of the house to Victorian families. It was the first place that visitors would see and so it was decorated in a way that would impress people.

The patterned floor tiles and the coloured glass in the doors can still be seen in Laurie's hall. The Browns would have hung up lots of pictures and might even have had a stuffed animal's head or a pair of antlers on the wall.

Bell

This bell is high up, near the ceiling. There is a piece of wire attached to it. Do you remember the little knob by the front door? The other end of the wire is fixed to the back of that knob. When a visitor arrives and pulls the knob, the wire is pulled and the bell jangles.

Bike

Laurie has a mountain bike. Mr Brown might have had a bike too. It could have looked a bit like this one. Air-filled tyres were only invented a few years before Mr Brown built this house. Before this, bicycle wheels were made from solid rubber.

The Parlour

This is the Pages' living room. It looks bright and airy. Can you see the television near the fireplace? Laurie likes watching sports programmes.

The Browns called this room the parlour. It was the best room in the house. It was only used on special occasions. Vera and Lily were never allowed to play in here.

Parlours often had lots of decoration. If you look closely at the photograph of Laurie's living room, you will see a pretty flower pattern around the edge of the ceiling.

The parlour also had the best fireplace in the house. The Browns' fireplace had an expensive marble surround. You can still see the surround in Laurie's living room. The wallpaper in the Browns' parlour had a heavy pattern and there were lots of pictures on the walls. Instead of having a television, they had a piano for entertainment.

Ornaments

This picture was taken at about the same time that Laurie's house was built. The Victorians loved ornaments and pictures.

Coal fires made the rooms very dusty. The maid would have had to dust each ornament every day!

Carved wood

During the Victorian Age woodcarving machines were invented. Before this, wood had to be carved by hand and only rich people could afford carved wood furniture. Late Victorian carved furniture still looked expensive but it was much cheaper to buy. Look at all the carving on this chair!

The Dining Room

Mary served all the Browns' meals in this room. The room was a bit less important than the parlour, so the fire surround was a little less grand too. Instead of being made of marble, it was made of slate. The Pages have painted the slate surround blue.

Victorian houses were often cold and draughty. Long, heavy curtains were usually hung at the windows to keep the draughts out.

The room was lit by oil lamps. Oil lamps gave out much less light than our modern electric bulbs. Dim lights, heavy curtains, patterned wallpaper and rooms crowded with furniture and ornaments made many Victorian houses look dark and gloomy.

The Pages use this room as a sitting room. Although the sofa is brightly coloured, the shape of all the furniture is quite plain.

Dresser

Victorian furniture was often quite ornate. As well as having lots of carving, this dresser has three mirrors and some fancy brass handles.

The Browns might have kept their best china in a dresser like this. Tablecloths and napkins would probably have been stored here too.

Lighting

This is called a ceiling rose. It is made of plaster. An oil or gas lamp would have hung below it. Much of the light from oil or gas lamps went upwards towards the ceiling. Instead of just lighting up a bare patch of ceiling, the lamp would have lit up this decoration.

The Kitchen

Laurie, Sam and Jan use this room as a dining room. The cupboard is Victorian but the smoke alarm on the ceiling certainly isn't!

Can you see the row of bells on the wall? Every room in the house had a bell pull. When the bell pull was pulled, it rang one of the bells in the kitchen. Mary could tell which room she was being called to by seeing which bell was ringing.

This is where Mary did all the cooking for the Brown family. Instead of having a gas or electric cooker as we have today, she used a range. A coal fire in the grate of the range heated up the ovens and the hot plates on the top. It also kept the kitchen nice and warm. Lily and Vera liked the kitchen. Sometimes Mary let them help her bake cakes.

Irons

This type of iron is called a flat iron. It was put onto the range to heat up. The maid worked with the iron until it got too cool to be any use and then put it back onto the range to heat up again. She would probably have used lots of irons so that as one iron was being used, others would be heating up.

Cooking equipment

This photograph was taken in a house that was much smaller than the Browns' house. The family who lived here cooked and lived in the same room. Can you spot the kettle hanging over the fire? You can just see two cats curled up in front of the range. One of them moved while the photograph was being taken and its head is a bit blurred.

The Scullery

Houses that were built at this time did not have electricity. In many Victorian homes all the hot water had to be heated on the range, but the Browns had a copper. You can see this in the corner of the scullery.

A copper was a large iron or copper boiler filled with water. A coal fire was lit under the boiler. This heated up the water.

This room is now the Pages' kitchen. Lots of the equipment is electric. Can you see an oven, a fridge-freezer and a microwave?

The sink was in the scullery and not in the kitchen. So, the washing up would have been done in here. It would not have been done by the Browns, of course, but by Mary. The sink was made of a type of pottery called stoneware. It had one cold tap. Mary had to carry the hot water over from the copper.

Laundry

The house where this photo was taken had two maids. The photo was taken outside the scullery. One maid is ironing while the other is washing clothes using a washing dolly in a tub. Usually they would have worked indoors. They probably went outside specially for the photograph.

Knife cleaner

Modern stainless steel knives stay clean and shiny. Most Victorian knives were made from ordinary steel, which stained very easily. Some households had a knife cleaner, like this one. The blades of the knives slotted into the machine. When the handle was turned, the blades were cleaned by moving parts inside the machine.

The Bathroom

You can see the Pages' washbasin and loo in this picture. There is a bath too, just past the washbasin.

Lots of Victorian families had to make do with an outdoor loo. But the Browns were lucky. They had a plumbed-in, upstairs loo.

Modern loos are close coupled. This means that the tank that holds the water is very close to the main part of the loo. The tanks of Victorian loos were high up on the wall, linked to the main part with a long pipe. A chain hung down from the tank. When it was pulled, the loo flushed. Some people today still call it "pulling the chain", even though we usually have to press a lever.

Victorian loos often had wooden seats. The one on the Pages' loo is actually the one that the Browns used!

Privies

In 1848 a law was passed saying that all homes had to have some sort of loo. Before this, what now goes down the loo was often just thrown out into the street gutters. Most people had a simple loo, like the one in this picture. It was called a privy and was usually in a little hut in the garden. The waste from the privy collected in a pit that had to be emptied.

Baths

During much of the Victorian Era, hot water for baths had to be brought from the copper or the range. Later, amazing machines were invented. Many had geysers over or near the bath. These geysers heated up water. They were really rather dangerous. Often the water that came out was actually boiling. Sometimes the geysers exploded and showered the bathroom with scalding hot water.

The Main Bedroom

Mr and Mrs Brown slept in a brass bed. Can you see the matching wardrobe, dressing table and chest of drawers? The Victorians would never have had built-in wardrobes in their bedrooms, as we do today.

There were fireplaces in all the bedrooms as well as in all the living rooms. Many Victorian fireplaces had pretty tiles inside the surround. If you look at the photograph of Laurie's bedroom you can still see the original Victorian tiles. Mr and Mrs Brown needed their coal fire to keep warm but Laurie's house has central heating. The fireplace is now just for decoration.

Laurie has this room as his bedroom. His bed has a wooden frame. Sometimes he listens to his personal stereo in bed.

Chaise longue

The piece of furniture at the end of the bed in this photograph is called a chaise longue. It has been covered with a furry rug.

A chaise longue is a cross between a sofa and a bed. You could lie back in the corner part of it with your feet stretched out along the seat.

What a lot of pictures there are in this room!

Jug and washbowl

Many Victorian bedrooms would have had a washstand with a jug and bowl on it. Even if a house had a bathroom, it may not have had a washbasin. So, a jug and a washbowl were used instead. The maid would have filled the jug with hot water from the kitchen or the scullery. Then she would have brought it up to the bedroom.

The Children's Room

Laurie's granny lives in America. She sleeps in this room when she visits. Jan uses the room to do her ironing too.

There was a large rug on the floor. Rugs were better than fitted carpets because they could be lifted up and taken outside to be cleaned. Mary would have hung the rug up outside and beaten it to knock out all the dust.

This was Vera and Lily's bedroom. There was a candle on the big chest underneath the bookshelves. Vera and Lily used to take turns blowing the candle out each night!

Under the bed you can see a chamber pot. Chamber pots were a bit like potties except that everyone, both children and adults, used them. It seems a strange idea to us now, but don't forget, most Victorians only had an outside loo.

Toys

Vera and Lily might have had a doll like this. She is made from porcelain. Porcelain is a type of pottery. She had to be played with carefully as porcelain breaks quite easily.

School

Vera and Lily both went to school. The school was only a few streets away. Their classroom might have looked like the one in the photograph. There were lots of children in this class and they all sat in rows, facing the front. The children in this class might have heard of America, where Laurie's granny lives, but they would probably never have met an American.

The Nursery

Baby Thomas and his nanny spent much of the day together in this room. They both slept in here too. A fireguard was put in front of the open fire to make sure there were no accidents. Can you see Thomas's wooden building blocks on the floor?

Some of the things in Jan's bedroom, such as the mirror and the plaster flowers on the ceiling, are Victorian. Others, like the electric lamp, are definitely modern.

Thomas's crib had lace frills and a lace canopy. It looked very pretty but it must have been difficult to wash and iron all that lace. When Mr Brown got home from work in the evening, Thomas was brought downstairs to see his parents for half an hour before being put to bed in his crib.

Prams

In the afternoons, Thomas's nanny used to take Thomas out for a walk in his pram. The pram might have looked like the one in this advert. Quite a lot of Victorian babies had nannies. The nannies would meet each other as they walked their babies through the park.

Screens

Victorians often had screens like this one in their bedrooms. They stood behind them to get dressed and undressed, just in case anyone came into the room! Can you see the picture of Queen Victoria on the middle section of the screen?

The Maid's Room

This is now Sam's bedroom. He has a duvet on his bed and a fitted carpet on his floor.

Instead of having duvets, Victorians had blankets and sheets. Mr and Mrs Brown had a thick, warm quilt on top of their blankets, but Mary only had a thin patchwork quilt on hers. Mr and Mrs Brown had an ornate brass bed but Mary had only a plain, narrow, iron bed.

This room was Mary's room. It was the smallest room in the house and had the tiniest fireplace. Most of the floor was just bare floorboards with one small rug by her bed. It looked very empty compared to the other bedrooms.

Polish

Mary needed lots of different polishes and cleaners. This one was used to polish the grates. Before laying the table and cooking and serving breakfast to the family, Mary had to clean out, polish, re-lay and light all the downstairs fires. Later, she had to do all the bedroom fires too.

A busy day

Many larger houses had three or four servants. Every day the maids had to move all the furniture in the rooms and sweep or beat the rugs. You can see two maids with a rug in the photograph. The little girl of the house is skipping.

All the furniture and ornaments in all the rooms had to be dusted too. During the day, maids polished the silver, cleaned the knives and did any washing, ironing and mending that was needed. As well as this, they had to cook and serve all the meals.

Things to Do

Stained Glass

The Victorians loved coloured, or stained, glass. You can make your own 'stained glass window' from black sugar paper and coloured tissue paper.

Cut the black sugar paper into whatever shape you would like. Then cut out lots of interesting shapes. Your window should now be full of holes!

Cover each hole with a piece of coloured tissue paper. Each piece should be slightly larger than the hole. Glue the tissue paper to the back of your window. Stick or hang your window in front of a clear glass window. The light will shine through the 'stained glass'.

Mosaic

The floor in the Pages' hall is made from lots of small coloured tiles that are arranged in a way that makes a pattern. This type of design is called mosaic.

You can make your own mosaic design using small shapes cut out of coloured, gummed paper stuck onto a piece of plain paper. Make sure that there are no gaps between the pieces of gummed paper.

You can design your own pattern or you could even try to make a picture of something, like a boat or a house.

Wallpaper

Lots of Victorian wallpaper was block printed. This means that a design was carved from a block of wood. The block was coated in ink and used to print the design all over the paper. You could print your own wallpaper design too. There are lots of different things you could use to print with. You could cut a sponge into a pretty shape and then dip it into a saucer of paint and print with it.

You could print with everyday objects like cotton reels or leaves. You could even make your own block prints by sticking shapes cut from thick cardboard onto small blocks of wood.

Glossary

architect	someone who designs buildings
brass	a shiny, yellow coloured metal
chaise longue	a type of sofa with a back rest only at one end
chamber pot	a type of pottery potty
copper	a large metal pot that water was boiled up in
crib	a baby's bed
draughty	when cold air blows into a room
geyser	a machine that heated up water
grate	a small metal basket that a fire was laid on
invention	a new object, machine or idea
nanny	a lady paid to look after babies and young children
ornate	fancy, with lots of decoration
plaster	a sand-based mixture that can be moulded or used to make a smooth surface on a wall
porcelain	a fine type of pottery
privy	an outdoor loo
quilt	a bed cover, often made from padded material
range	a type of cooker
scalding	very hot
steel	a metal that is mostly made of iron
stoneware	a rough type of pottery
stucco	plaster that covers an outside wall
terrace	a row of houses that are joined together
Victorian	anything that lived or was made between 1837 and 1901
washing dolly	a wooden object that looked like a short stool with a long handle, for moving the washing about in the washing tub.

Index